CAST YOUR CARE

The Key to Harvest

CAST YOUR CARE

The Key to Harvest

Carolyn Chambers

Cast Your Care – The Key to Harvest
Carolyn Chambers
© Copyright 2017 by Carolyn Chambers. All rights reserved. Unless otherwise indicated, all scripture quotations are taken from the King James Version of the Bible.

No portion of this book may be reproduced, stored in a retrieval system or transmitted in any form electronic, mechanical, photocopy, recording or any other except for brief quotations in printed reviews, without prior consent of the publisher.

Library of Congress
Cataloging-in-Publication Data

Cast Your Care – The Key to Harvest
Printed in the United States of America
ISBN: 978-099675823-9

Cover design by CW Technology Consulting

www.anointedlifepublishing.com

Contents

Introduction ix
Chapter 1 Care Keeps the Attack There .. 1
Chapter 2 Care Must Be Answered 13
Chapter 3 Care Causes Defeat 27
Chapter 4 Cultivating Joy 37
Chapter 5 The Harvest-Due Season 45
Salvation Prayer 61
About the Author 63

Special thanks to my editor and husband, Keith, whose gifts and anointing made this book come alive. He continues to take the ordinary and turn it into the extraordinary. It is his contribution to the book that enables the reader to become established.

I will speak, that I may be refreshed: I will open my lips and answer.

(Job 32:20)

Introduction

Care is a mechanism that once it's engaged, it dogs our trail.

A few years ago, my niece found herself on the way to work, driving on the freeway, only to be turned around with the care of: *Did I turn off the stove?* Time after time, when the attack occurred, she would turn around, go back and check. One time, she had gotten all the way to the other side of town and had to turn around. Each time there was no need for alarm.

By understanding the mechanism of care, she began resisting it. And by remaining steadfast, today she is free.

Care is a weapon of the flesh. Although we are called to occupy, no two objects can occupy the same space at the same time. As human beings, we are either in our spirit or in our flesh, depending on the thoughts we receive.

When we are in the spirit, we are led by faith; even knowing the end from the beginning. However, when we are in our flesh (our lower nature), we are led by care. And care keeps us out of the will of God. Being in the dark, it questions everything and can't hold its peace.

The strength of care is hidden behind the power of thought: *"For as he thinketh in his heart, so is he,"* (Proverbs 23:7).

Our thoughts of care become building blocks to construct 'weapons,' which the enemy uses against us, whether they are negative thinking patterns, misperceptions, or imaginations that exalt themselves against the knowledge of God. Moreover, it has been said, that we will arrive at the place of our thoughts, *whether they are good or bad.*

As thoughts of care are received, the enemy says: *"Eat and drink,"* (Proverbs 23:7). Translation: think your care and speak your care. It goes on to say: *"...but his heart is not with thee."* For when we receive care, we suffer needless loss of peace. And, because care is pleasant to the soul (agreeable to the senses), we typically don't resist it. Yet, thoughts of care should be handled with discretion (the ability to judge critically), for only then are we preserved.

While talking with one of my daughters, she shared a concern about her future, stating that her biological clock was ticking. Although she is a woman of faith, in the area of her care, thoughts had formed a stronghold—a weapon that had effectively stolen her joy. To make matters worse, she was having difficulty getting 'around' the construct that she had built. You could call it a house of care. Because the care was pleasant (it made sense), she yielded to it. Yet, it was an attack that was causing her lots of emotional pain.

I shared with her the revelation regarding care that the Holy Spirit had given me, particularly: "Your care is keeping the attack there. The key to harvest is to cast your care."

It is important to know that the attack is primarily against the fruit of the Spirit; the only weapon that can effectively keep the flesh at bay.

The flesh uses care to disrupt the fruit-bearing process of love, joy, peace, patience, kindness, goodness, faith, meekness and temperance. The flesh attacks through any area of strong desire. In my daughter's case, it was the pressure of her biological clock ticking. *Care* was found in the area where there should have been *patience* (that virtue that does not surrender to circumstances or succumb under trials).

Once she heard that revelation, without hesitation, her response was, "You need to write that book!" And she was off the phone. I pondered her words, and I finally agreed—realizing that the power of this revelation had *immediately* set her free, as it had also done for me.

I believe that the reader, too, will be enlightened and blessed as the anointing of this revelation makes a demand on your heart, in uprooting care.

In Deuteronomy 9:3, God promises to bring them [enemies] down before our face, so that we shall drive them out and destroy them, quickly. This book helps in the fulfilment of that promise.

"...for the prince of this world cometh, and hath nothing in me."

(John 14:30)

Chapter 1

Care Keeps the Attack There

A few days after Christmas, my brother (who lives with me) had a reaction to one of his medications. It had dropped his blood sugar to a dangerous level, and the side effects mimicked those of a stroke. He had been taking communion (twice a day) so I knew it was not a stroke. Nevertheless, because of the symptoms, we took him to the emergency room. His MRI was normal, as well as all the other tests. They changed his medication and released him, but I *was* told to monitor him.

I prayed for him to receive his healing. And, although I believed he was healed, I continued to check his blood sugar, as directed. That night I was awakened every two to three hours with the care of checking his blood sugar; each time the levels were unstable. So, I found myself encouraging him to eat something to bring it back into normal range. But to make matters worse, he didn't have an appetite, so the problem was compounded.

This pattern continued well into the next day. Interestingly enough, in my heart I knew he was healed, yet the levels continued to fluctuate. Needless to say, I was alarmed and dreaded spending another sleepless night worried about his sugar dropping to a dangerously low level again.

That's when the Holy Spirit spoke to me and said, "The care is keeping the attack there." He went on to say, "The key to harvest is to cast your care."

Care Keeps the Attack There

I responded immediately! I began to cast my care and stopped the excessive monitoring.

That night is when the test came. I was again awakened several times with the care of checking his blood sugar. This time I responded, thinking: *The care keeps the attack there*. And each time I went back to sleep. Even realizing how dangerous a drop in his blood sugar could be, I refused to take on that care, again. Care must be cast, even legitimate care.

Care can be described as the pressure of the circumstance—the concern or the anxiety. And, very often, care manifests as shame, guilt, pain, unforgiveness, frustration, or even anger. We must manage the situation, while standing against the pressure of that situation.

The casting of care is akin to removing scales from a fish or dross from silver. For us, as individuals, it involves the renewing of the mind.

It has now been over six months since my brother's attack; his doctor has even reduced his blood sugar medication. And his blood sugar continues to be within the normal range, whether he eats or not. His doctor called it 'controlled.'

The Enemy Returns

It happens often, that once we have received our deliverance, or our healing, there is the concern of the symptoms returning, or of a relapse. This threat, fueled by care, could potentially put us in harm's way. Unless the care is cast, the threat is real.

After God delivered the children of Israel out of Egypt, Pharaoh was not pleased with the fact that the slaves had been set free. So, he and his six hundred men came after them. According to the Bible, they said: *"Why have we done this, that we have let Israel go from serving us,"* (Exodus 14:5). The goal of the enemy was to steal their peace. This could not be accomplished without the presence of care.

Because the children of Israel failed to cast their care back in Egypt, their care followed them and became a threat. The Bible said: *"...and they were sore afraid... And they said unto Moses ...Is <u>not this the word</u> that we did tell you in Egypt, saying, Let us alone, that we may serve the Egyptians? For it had been better for us to serve the Egyptians, than that we should die in the wilderness,"* (Exodus 14:11-12).

Moses instructed them to: *"...fear not, stand still...The LORD shall fight for you, and ye shall hold your peace."* Care loses it power in the presence of the fruit of peace. After receiving the Word of promise, they cast their care. Now God could eliminate the threat completely, and He did.

Care Keeps the Attack There

The Care Alert

The principle of casting your care is found in 1 Peter 5. Peter tells us what to do, why we must do it, and how to do it:

What: *"Likewise you younger people, submit yourselves to your elders. Yes, all of you be submissive to one another, and be clothed with humility,*

Why: *for God resists the proud, But gives grace to the humble. Therefore humble yourselves under the mighty hand of God, that He may exalt you in due time,*

How: *casting all your care upon Him, for He cares for you,"* 1 Peter 5:5-7 (NKJV).

Those with care are filled with pride (leaning to their own understanding) and are being resisted, not helped by God.

The Sober Alert

Peter goes on to tells us what will happen if we don't cast our care:

What: *"Be sober, be vigilant;*

Why: *because your adversary the devil walks about like a roaring lion, seeking whom he may devour.*

How: *Resist him, steadfast in the faith, knowing that the same sufferings are experienced by your brotherhood in the world,"* (1 Peter 5:8-9 NKJV).

Unless care is resisted by faith, your adversary, the devil, can devour (ruin the soul, destroy) those with care.

Care Keeps the Attack There

Care Awakens the Lion

A couple was enjoying a nice evening walk when the decision was made to stop at a nearby fast food joint for a quick bite to eat. The man allowed his wife to peaceably place her order. However, as he began to place *his* order, she, being filled with care, usurped his authority by questioning his choice. Thinking out loud, she suggested to him what she thought was a more suitable item on the menu, one that he had eaten often. Reflexively, he 'snapped' at her. She jumped back, puzzled, asking herself what she had done wrong.

As she shared the story with me, God gave me a vision of a lion, who had been asleep, who suddenly awakened with a roar! The wife's pride was being resisted and what she perceived as being helpful was, in effect, a care. This care should have been cast.

When we operate in care, directing our care toward others, we fail to realize that the other person can't listen to us and to the Holy Spirit at the same time. We can't serve two masters. Her husband was attempting to walk by faith. Her care tried to disrupt that fruit-bearing process. The key is to cast your care, and hold your peace.

Care Keeps the Attack There

The Guard Alert

Care and peace can't occupy the same space at the same time. For this reason we are admonished to guard the heart:

What: *"Keep your heart with all diligence,*
Why: *For out of it spring the issues of life.*
How: *Put away from you a deceitful mouth, and put perverse lips far from you,"* (Proverbs 4:23-24 NKJV).

The heart is guarded by casting our care. The fruit of the Spirit must be allowed to flow out of our hearts and not be *blocked* by thoughts of care. When guarded, these fruit war against the deceitful mouth and perverse lips of the flesh.

"...behold, I say unto you, Lift up your eyes, and look on the fields; for they are white already to harvest."

(John 4:35)

Chapter 2

Care Must Be Answered

A young lady, who was in the process of starting her ministry, asked her mom for one hundred dollars to buy a Bible. Although she already owned several Bibles, her favorite one needed to be replaced. But her mom refused to give her the money, so she was disappointed.

Later on, during a telephone conversation with me, she shared the expense of starting her ministry and the need for an additional two hundred and fifty dollars. Naturally, I suggested that she ask her mom. She shared her care, stating that her mom had refused to buy her a Bible for one hundred dollars, so surely she would refuse to give her two hundred and fifty dollars. I answered the care, thinking to myself: *My mom would give me the money to help with my ministry*, and I believed her mom would do the same.

Not sharing my reasoning with her, I suggested that she ask her mom anyway. She did. And her mom was more than happy to help her…asking her how soon she would need the money. Feeling overjoyed, this young lady couldn't figure out what had just happened. I explained to her that I had answered her care, and without care the enemy could not devour.

When care is answered, virtue is released, and the power of God flows. This is why the Bible says, in Proverbs 15:23, a man has joy by the answer of his mouth.

The Fields Are White

Care often comes in the form of questions. They seem benign, but they are from the realm of the flesh, being void of life and peace. Even in the Garden of Eden, the serpent began with a question: *"...Has God indeed said, 'You shall not eat of every tree of the garden?'"* (Genesis 3:1 NKJV).

The flesh is attempting to get us to walk by sight...speaking our philosophy: feelings, opinions, fears, doubts, unbelief, and concerns. According to the Bible, we are spoiled (rendered useless) by our philosophy and vain deceit.

It is our philosophy that keeps us in the *field* (a type of flesh), alienated from the fruit of the Spirit. And, without fruit, the field can be a dangerous place to be in. Remember, Abel was killed in the field, and the elder brother of the prodigal son was angry in the field. But, in John 4, Jesus said that the fields were white. I was intrigued. What had changed?

John explains it in the story of Jesus speaking to a Samaritan woman at the well. Being weary in His journey, He addressed the problem of care: *"<u>Jesus said to her</u>, "Give Me a drink,"* (John 4 NKJV).

The woman responded with care—questioning Jesus' motive: *"Then the woman of Samaria said to Him, "How is it that You, being a Jew, ask a drink from me, a Samaritan woman?" For Jews have no dealings with Samaritans."*

As all care must be answered, Jesus responded by sowing seeds of life and peace. The Bible said: "Jesus <u>answered</u> and <u>said to her</u>, *"If you knew the gift of God, and who it is who says to you, 'Give Me a drink,' you would have asked*

Care Must Be Answered

Him, and He would have given you living water."

But, not being fully persuaded, she questioned Him again, by sharing another care: *"The woman said to Him, "Sir, You have nothing to draw with, and the well is deep. Where then do You get that living water? Are You greater than our father Jacob, who gave us the well, and drank from it himself, as well as his sons and his livestock?"*

Continuing to sow seeds of life and peace, *"Jesus <u>answered</u> and <u>said to her</u>, "Whoever drinks of this water will thirst again, but whoever drinks of the water that I shall give him will never thirst. But the water that I shall give him will become in him a fountain of water springing up into everlasting life."*

Finally, after casting the whole of her care, *"The woman said to Him, "Sir, give me this water, that I may not thirst, nor come here to draw."*

She was now walking by faith, seeing things from God's perspective; echoing the Master's words. This time Jesus did not have to answer—for she was free of care. The Bible said: *"Jesus said unto her…"* Basically, Jesus could now talk to her *face to face*. There was no more care standing between them to be answered.

This woman was a seeker, but her care kept her limited to the natural realm. Casting her care, she received a breakthrough. She now had the liberty to receive the wisdom of God unhindered by care. The seed (the incorruptible Word), spoken by Jesus, had made a demand on the soil of her heart. She was now clean through the Word that had been spoken to her. (John 15:3) Jesus had taken every thought captive. (2 Corinthians 10:5)

Afterwards, Jesus told his disciples that the fields were *white for harvest*. He had overcome evil with good.

Later, while ministering to a certain nobleman in that same chapter, Jesus <u>proved</u> that the fields were now white for harvest and that care had been eradicated once and for all. The nobleman came to Jesus seeking healing for his son. He certainly had a problem (his son was near death), but care was absent. Jesus even tested the man's faith and found him to be free of care—now His disciples could see for themselves that the fields were now white for harvest.

With no care to answer, <u>Jesus said unto him</u>, *"Go your way; your son lives."* When we are free of care, the power of God flows; God's Word has free course.

Carolyn Chambers

The Power of the Last Word Spoken

Words are designed to produce after themselves—they will produce either life or death. They will yield either blessings or curses. The last word spoken turns the tide of the battle. When Jesus got the last word in, the Samaritan woman was converted, and the nobleman's son was healed.

In fighting care, we must make sure that the last words that come out of our mouths are words of life and peace.

Poor Reception

The Holy Spirit gave my husband, Keith, an increase on the revelation of care: He shared that when challenges are encountered in the natural, which can be resolved within our own strength, care is not usually an issue. However, when the problem is beyond our ability and supernatural help is needed, care arises to disrupt our communication with God. Similar to static on the line in a telephone call, care creates receptivity issues causing the answer to our prayers to be hindered.

No Excuse for Failure

In Matthew 25, the *parable of the talents* speaks of three servants who were each given one to five talents (by their Lord), according to their ability. In other words, He did not put more on them than they were able to handle. Being fair and generous, He also gave them a long time to produce.

The first two did not disappoint Him. Using their talents, they produced according to the trust bestowed upon them. They were profitable servants. Speaking to each one directly: *"<u>His lord said to him</u>, Well done, good and faithful servant; you were faithful over a few things, I will make you ruler over many things. Enter into the joy of your lord."*

Finding the first two free of care, they were praised, promoted, and allowed to enter into the joy of the Lord. However, the servant who had received one talent failed to produce. Being in the flesh, he could only <u>focus</u> on his care—he had failed to guard his heart.

When it was reckoning time, he gave his Lord lots of excuses and consequently received a rebuke. The Bible said: *"His Lord <u>answered</u> and <u>said unto him</u>, You wicked and lazy servant… Take the talent from him…"* His Lord <u>answered his care</u>; however, because there was *no excuse* for his failure, his talent was taken from him.

This servant failed to realize that all servants were anointed to overcome; even Jesus said He also had to overcome- it's what we do, as was proven by the other two servants. His excuses rendered him unprofitable (useless). So, he was <u>cast</u> into outer darkness, the place of care. He received no praise and no promotion. His reward was stolen by care.

Legitimate Care Answered

In 2 Kings 4, the story is told of a Shunammite woman whose son had died. But she remained in faith—free of care. She refused to speak even her legitimate care. Instead, she answered the care herself by establishing her position and remaining steadfast. Taking her stand, she asked her husband to prepare for her one of the donkeys that she may go to the man of God: *"So he said, "Why are you going to him today? It is neither the New Moon nor the Sabbath."*

She refused to speak care. Her answer was: "*It shall be well.*"

When the man of God saw her afar off, he told his servant to run and ask her: *"Is it well with her? Is it well with her husband? Is it well with the child?"*

"And she <u>answered</u>, It is well."

Care Must Be Answered

Her answer to care was: It shall be well, it is well. And with this response, you could say that her field was white. Now a miracle could take place. The man of God prayed for her son, and his life returned to him.

Speaking her care would have contaminated her faith and hindered the healing process. The confession: It shall be well; it is well, addresses a variety of care. And it works every time. However, unwavering consistency is the key.

Carolyn Chambers

O Israel: thou canst not stand before thine enemies, until ye take away the accursed thing from among you.

(Joshua 7:13)

Chapter 3

Care Causes Defeat

When care comes in the form of things we strongly desire, it hinders our ability to stand before our enemies. After conquering Jericho, the children of Israel set out to conquer the next town, called Ai. It was a small country and they assumed that they would easily defeat it. But when they tried, they were beaten. Bewildered, they sought an answer from God. He told them what the problem was…someone had violated the covenant and had taken of the accursed things. (Joshua 7) Care was in the camp.

They found out that the culprit was a young man by the name of Achan. He confessed his sin stating that he had found some things in Jericho that he coveted and hid them in his tent. These were things he cared about. His actions grieved God because it is the Word that should be hidden in our hearts, not things.

According to Mark 4, the cares of this world was one of three factors that chokes the word of God and it becomes unfruitful.

Being found with care, Achan and his family were stoned; God then spoke and assured Joshua saying that, *"… you shalt do to Ai and her king as you didst unto Jericho and her king…"* They obeyed, and Ai was defeated.

Care Causes Defeat

Unanswered Care

About three months ago my husband and I had pavers put in our backyard to make a walk path. As the layout was being drawn up, I questioned one section. I wanted to make sure that there would be enough room for a walker or a wheel chair. Because it was a sincere care, I didn't think about casting it. I even asked the landscaper, who measured all the areas, to assure me that particular area would be fine, and he did. Yet, as care so often does, it continued to dog my trail.

After the work was completed, one area seemed to be smaller. It was the area of my care. When I measured the space, it was narrower than the other three areas that were free of care. Suddenly, I realized my error. I did not cast my care and it kept the attack there; so the harvest suffered.

    Some would say that I was simply proven correct. But this line of thinking fails to realize that it was my care that created the problem in the first place. Without care, all areas would have been flawless. Remember, you will arrive at the place of your thoughts, *whether they are good or bad*—as a man thinks in his heart, so is he. To war against self-fulfilling prophesies coming to pass, we need to cast our care.

    After falling prey to care, the Bible says we must *count it all joy*. Why this is necessary is explained in James 1:2-4.

The Count It All Joy Alert

What: *"My brethren, count it all joy when ye fall into various trials;*
Why: *Knowing this, that the testing of your faith produces patience.*
How: *But let patience have its perfect work, that you may be perfect and complete, lacking nothing,"* (James 1:2-4).

In counting it all joy, we are declaring the end from the beginning; giving faith something to work with. Joy is needed to see the end of our faith, even the salvation of our souls. Paul calls it the joy of faith.

I counted the mishap with the pavers all joy and received peace. Consequently, I can now expect one of four outcomes: a reversal of the curse, a turnaround, a restoration, or a better resurrection.

Carolyn Chambers

Care Attacks Joy

Recently I was confronted with a situation that riddled me with care. It came as a threat against my son's college GPA. It could mean the loss of a scholarship as well as future ramifications. This care effectively stole my joy. Although I had spent hours in prayer, and he experienced lots of victories, yet he appeared to have missed his GPA goal by a few points. So, I asked the Holy Spirit how I should handle the situation. He said, "Count it all joy." So I did. And I also asked for wisdom to see where he had missed it.

Later, I noticed that I still felt a sense of sadness. So I asked Him what else I should do. He said, "Stand" (in joy). I said, "OK." So I stood. What's interesting is that for the rest of that day and the next, my countenance was no

Care Causes Defeat

more sad, even though the circumstances had not changed.

I also noticed that the atmosphere in my house had changed for the better—there was a sense of joy. That piqued my interest. Then, I was promptly reminded by the Holy Spirit what happens when we stand in the place of our authority. According to Judges 7, when we stand, the enemy runs, cries, and flees. The enemy is defenseless in the absence of care.

God's Wisdom

After counting it all joy, the Bible says if any man lack wisdom let him ask of God who gives it to him liberally. (James 1:5) In showing my son where he had missed it, God led me to Jeremiah 10:23: *"O LORD, I know that the way of man is not in himself: it is not in man that walks to direct his steps."* It seemed my son had been directing his own steps.

And, the next morning, during our devotions, we also read Proverbs 3:5-6, that stated: *"Trust in the LORD with all thine heart; and lean not unto thine own understanding. In all thy ways acknowledge him, and he shall direct thy paths."*

Being convicted by these scriptures, my son realized that he had not only been directing his own steps, but he

Care Causes Defeat

had also been leaning to his own understanding and not acknowledging God.

My son said, "You think you are exercising your own independence, yet it is a set-up for failure."

After our devotions, we reviewed all the problems he had encountered that semester and counted it all joy. Then we prepared for our turnaround.

Although the GPA was stolen, the Holy Spirit reminded me: 'If the enemy can't steal your joy, he can't keep your goods.' We then realized that it was time to look forward to a better resurrection.

Three months later, my son received three new scholarships. One of which, doubled the amount of the one that was stolen!

Carolyn Chambers

"...even all the trees of the field, are withered: because joy is withered away from the sons of men."

(Joel 1:12)

Chapter 4

Cultivating Joy

When my brother-in-law, Mario, went home to be with the Lord, I tried to encourage his teenage son but found myself full of sorrowful care. I just couldn't shake it. I kept trying to reach my joy but sorrow kept interrupting me. Without joy, I had no strength and no presence of God. I could not minister in that state of mind.

So I tried harder and harder, even leaping for joy and jumping for joy. Finally, sorrow left. I was able to finish my conversation, and he was thoroughly blessed by it. However, because it was such a tough attack, I feared it would return. Then the Holy Spirit said to me, "No, it will not return." And it didn't.

When we stand in the place of our authority, the Bible says the enemy fears being stoned again. So he runs, cries, and flees. By taking my stand, I had defeated the enemy with joy.

Care and joy can't occupy the same space at the same time. Joy, being defined as a calm delight, is an antidote that enables us to see the end of our faith. It is designed to bring *strength* to the situation at hand; the expectation of good.

Joy is also an offensive weapon; it places the ball in our court. It is needed to draw water out of the well of salvation to receive healing, wholeness, deliverance, and prosperity.

It is the presence or absence of joy that determines whether we will serve God or serve the enemy. In Matthew 25, ten virgins went forth to meet the Bridegroom; five were wise and five were foolish. The foolish took no oil with them, but the wise took oil (a type of joy) in their vessels; they had joy in the Holy Ghost—even joy unspeakable. To buy the fruit of joy, the wise virgins sold all fear, doubt, unbelief, and care. They were ready to be blessed. At the midnight hour, it was joy that brought the Bridegroom to them; they went in and the door was shut. Not having joy, the other five virgins could not serve God.

    This is also what Jonah realized while he was in the belly of the whale. He could have served the enemy by observing lying vanities; instead he chose to serve God with the voice of thanksgiving, and he was delivered. It is the voice of joy that causes the Lord to return the captivity of the land, for joy reverses the curse.

Carolyn Chambers

It's in the Bag

Several years ago, during bedtime, I was plagued by routine care. Thoughts such as: *Tomorrow you will have to do it again. You don't have an exciting life. You get up and pray, take care of the children, go to work, come home, and do it all over again.*

Although this attack occurred for a number of nights, I didn't answer the care, believing that it was true. Then the Holy Spirit spoke saying, "It's in the bag."

So, as an obedient child of God, I responded, "It's in the bag." I felt peace immediately.

Since that time, God would show me visions of garbage bags, labeled and categorized. There was a bag for *unbelief*, a bag for *doubt*, a bag for *pride*, and of late, even a bag for the *natural (sight)*.

However, the other day, I was delightfully awakened to a vision of another trash bag. It was categorized as *care*. It was full and about to be taken out …no pun intended. I then realized that the whole of my care: past, present, and future had been cast, once and for all. It is a part of my redemptive rest. Throughout that day, care would come and I would joyfully answer: "It's in the bag."

Taunts of Care

My husband shared his own observation of his interaction with taunts of care—that is, if he found himself forgetting about a disturbing situation, it was a sign that there was nothing to worry about. He would often say to me, "You know, I forgot about that…," he would add, "that's a good sign."

And, he is remarkably accurate. When I sought to analyze this amazing insight of knowing when there was nothing to worry about, the Holy Spirit said, "Because it was already in the bag."

Cultivating Joy

Casting Care

Years ago, God gave my husband a dream showing him what happens when we cast our care. My husband said the enemy would give him piles of stuff, ugly stuff. Each time, my husband would take the ugly stuff and turn it over to God. God would then take that same stuff and transform it into something beautiful. This happened several times before he awakened from the dream.

Philippians 4:6-7, explains the process: *"Be careful for nothing; but in everything by prayer and supplication with thanksgiving let your requests be made known unto God. And the peace of God, which passeth all understanding, shall keep your hearts and minds through Christ Jesus."*

Prayer: Father, I cast the whole of my care upon You. I give You praise and receive Your peace. Amen.

Carolyn Chambers

"...for Jordan overflows all his banks all the time of harvest..."

(Joshua 3:15)

Chapter 5

The Harvest-Due Season

One lady had been dealing with issues against her mother for over forty years. Within the last two years, she was delivered, having reconciled with her mother. Nevertheless, lately, she found herself embroiled in more conflicts.

Not realizing that the enemy had returned, to bring her back into bondage, she was bewildered—thinking that she had put such things behind her. She found herself accusing her mom of being insensitive to her own needs. And each accusation against her mom increased in severity; fueling her resentment.

Being vexed by anxious thoughts day to day, she wished she could just stay away from her; that would solve a lot of her problems. But, because her mom was elderly and had several health challenges, her help was desperately needed. She questioned why God had put her in such a difficult situation.

Finally, I suggested that she see all the different issues against her mother as cares. And, to keep it simple, she was directed to see each issue as a letter of the Care Alphabet: Care A—my mom can do some things for herself. Care B—she's not telling the truth. Care C—she doesn't care that *my* back hurts too, and so on. Eventually, she got the point and followed my instructions.

As an issue arose, she found herself saying, "It's one of the Care ABCs.

The Harvest-Due Season

To another issue she would say, "That's one of the alphabets, too."

Finally, she fully realized that what had appeared to be issues, that she had been harboring, were actually all cares.

The next day, God gave her a *vision* showing that she had conquered all her care; and in that vision, nothing her mom said or did offended her. As each care manifested, she humbled herself by submitting to her mom's natural request; however, spiritually she was humbling herself under the mighty hand of God.

While still in the vision, she was encouraged by a soft voice behind her saying: "That care is in the alphabet also." And that care was conquered. Cares that had usually 'set her off,' meant nothing to her. In the spirit, she had no problem serving her mom.

That same evening the *actual* test of care came, and she passed with flying colors. She was able to perform each task, in caring for her mother, with joy.

Also, taking the time to answer each care, which was her confession of faith, prepared her for due season. This was harvest time. The field was white. And she was free.

Her mom, upon recognizing the difference in her disposition toward her, rewarded her handsomely.

The Harvest-Due Season

Casting Care Releases Finances

My sister had fallen into a bout of depression, being devastated following the arrest of her son. To make matters worse, she was in need of ten thousand dollars for his release. There was no natural hope, so care came in like a flood—giving her no rest for her soul. She was grief strickened. I instructed her to take the word of God and war a mighty warfare against care.

Using the scripture found in Isaiah 54:17: *"No weapon formed against me shall prosper, every tongue that shall rise up against me in judgment, I shall condemn. This is my inheritance, and my righteousness is of the Lord,"* she began her warfare. Resisting care day and night, she gave God no rest. Fighting back floods of tears, each word of this passage became a weapon against her care. She fought vehemently for her inheritance, spiritually condemning every voice of judgment, with all her might. The enemy never knew what hit him. Finally, two weeks later, the money came in, and her son was released. He is now a college graduate.

As an enemy of faith, care keeps us in the natural realm—the area of its dominion. In a veil of secrecy, using either past cares, present cares, or future cares, the flesh manipulates our sense knowledge with the intent of stopping the work of faith. The Bible says in Nehemiah 4:11: *"...our adversaries said, They shall not know, neither see, till we come in the midst among them, and slay them, and cause the work to cease."*

The slaying ceases when the enemy hears words of faith—he knows you are not walking by sight (sense knowledge). The snare is broken. He flees.

The Harvest-Due Season

It is care that keeps the attack against faith going on in our lives. So, the key to harvest is to cast our care. Harvest involves the process of due season…the ability to endure till the end. We must stand against care as we would stand against any other attacks on our spirit, soul, or body.

Jesus declared that the fields were white and ready for harvest. And, on the cross, He declared that the redemptive work was finished; this work includes rest from care. When care is resisted, you enter into the finished work known also as due season: the promise to reap if we faint not.

In casting our care, I have found that the Prayer of Thanksgiving is an effective weapon that helps us endure till the end. The following prayers will help you in that process. It is time to cast *your* care.

Carolyn Chambers

"There remaineth therefore a rest to the people of God."

(Hebrews 4:9)

The Harvest-Due Season

Prayers of Thanksgiving
Against Care Relative to Children

I thank You, Father, that You have made me a joyful mother of children.

I thank You, Father, that my seed shall be mighty in the land.

I thank You, Father, that my seed shall possess the gate of the enemy.

I thank You, Father, that my children are taught of the Lord and great shall be the peace of my children.

I thank You, Father, that You gave me five talents and I have gained five more.

I thank You, Father, that my children are overcomers and more than conquerors.

Carolyn Chambers

Prayers of Thanksgiving
Against Care Relative to Finances

I thank You, Father, that my meal barrel shall not run dry neither shall my cruse of oil fail.

I thank You, Father, that in my prosperity I shall never be moved, and in the days of famine I shall be satisfied.

I thank You, Father, that I have a full provision and an abundance supply.

I thank You, Father, that You shall supply all of my need according to Your riches in glory through Christ Jesus. I thank You, Father, that You look ahead and make provision for me. I thank You, Father, that I shall prosper, continue prospering until I have greatly prospered.

The Harvest-Due Season

Prayers of Thanksgiving
Against Care Relative to Circumstances

I thank You, Father, that in all these things I am more than a conqueror.

I thank you, Father, that You cause my enemies that rise up against me to be defeated before my face, they will come out against me one way but flee from before me seven ways.

I thank you, Father, that You spoiled principalities and powers and made a show of them openly, triumphing over them in it.

I thank you, Father, that no weapon that is formed against me shall prosper; and every tongue that shall rise against me in judgment I shalt condemn.

Carolyn Chambers

**Prayers of Thanksgiving
Against Care Relative to Relationships**

I thank You, Father, that love takes no account of evil done to it, and pays no attention to a suffered wrong.

I thank You, Father, that love covers a multitude of sins.

I thank You, Father, that he who is without sin cast the first stone. I thank You Father that he who loves the Father loves the son also.

I thank You, Father, that we love one another as You have loved us. I thank You, Father, that we put on bowels of mercy, humbleness of mind, forgiving one another. We put on love, the bond of perfection.

The Harvest-Due Season

**Prayers of Thanksgiving
Against Care Relative to Unforgiveness**

I thank You, Father, that if I don't forgive others neither will my Father in heaven forgive me.

I thank You, Father, that You have separated my sins as far as the east is from the west. And that You will not remember them anymore.

I thank You, Father, that when my brother sin against me, I shall forgive him seven times seven.

I thank You, Father, that I owe no man nothing but love.

I thank You, Father, that I do unto others as I would have them do unto me.

Carolyn Chambers

**Prayers of Thanksgiving
Against Care Relative to Your Peace**

I thank You, Father, that I have peace like a river. Peace be still, Peace be still.

I thank You, Father, that You have delivered my soul in peace from the battle that was against me.

I thank You, Father, that I have the peace of God that surpasses all understanding, shall guard my heart and mind through Christ Jesus.

I thank You, Father, that I think on things that are true, honest, just, pure, lovely, and of a good report. If there be any virtue or praise, I think on these things.

The Harvest-Due Season

**Prayer of Thanksgiving
Against Care Relative to Relapse**

I thank You, Father, that the affliction shall not rise up the second time.

I thank You, Father, that the enemy has no healing of his bruise and his wound is grievous.

I thank You, Father, that You have set a bound that they cannot pass over; they come not again to cover the earth.

I thank You, Father, her mightiest warriors no longer fight. They stay in their barracks, their courage gone. They have become like women. (NLT)

I thank You, Father, that the fields are white, ready for harvest.

That if thou shalt confess with thy mouth the Lord Jesus, and shalt believe in thine heart that God hath raised him from the dead, thou shalt be saved. For with the heart man believeth unto righteousness; and with the mouth confession is made unto salvation.

(Romans 10:9-10)

Salvation Prayer

Father, I believe that Jesus is the Son of God. And that He was raised from the dead for my justification. Jesus, come into my heart and take over my life; be my Lord and Savior. Your Word says: Ask and you shall receive. For everyone who asks receives. I believe I receive You now in Jesus Name, Amen.

Now therefore ye are no more strangers and foreigners, but fellowcitizens with the saints, and of the household of God.

(Ephesians 2:19)

About the Author

Carolyn Chambers is a licensed minister and a member of Faith Ministerial Alliance. She is a celebrated Christian author, and is best known for her groundbreaking work: *Discovering Your Anointing Numbers: Allow me to introduce you to Yourself.*

She and her husband, Keith, have also developed Anointing Profiles that yield personalized commentaries based on birth demographics.

Carolyn holds a Bachelor's degree from the University of Wisconsin and a Master's degree from the University of Arizona. She and her husband live in Phoenix, Arizona, with their two sons: Nehemiah and Zacharias. They are members of Pilgrim Rest Baptist Church.

Other Books by Carolyn Chambers

DISCOVERING YOUR ANOINTING NUMBERS

Carolyn Chambers

In her life-changing new book, Carolyn Chambers helps readers discover their anointing numbers and empower them to fight life's great battle-themselves. Simply put—everyone is at war with *self*. But walking anointed is something everyone can achieve. In, "Discovering Your Anointing Numbers: Allow me to introduce you to Yourself," Carolyn Chambers examines the influence that birth demographics have on human behavior. This is a compelling read for all.

THE ANOINTED LIFE- *Crucifying the Flesh*

Carolyn Chambers

The Anointed Life: **Powerful New Book by Celebrated Christian Author Proves Flesh is the True "Enemy of the Soul"**

Everyone faces adversity and tests in life; but some pass where others fail. While faith and the word of God explain why these patterns exist, millions still search for answers. In her compelling new book, the author exposes the true enemy of the soul – the flesh. "Simply put," she says, "everybody is at war with themselves."

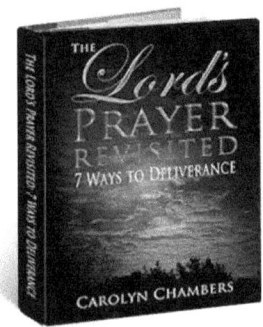

THE LORD'S PRAYER -- REVISITED

7 WAYS TO DELIVERENCE

Carolyn Chambers

Praying the Lord's Prayer is the Answer Understanding The Lord's Prayer is the Solution!

Understanding is the key to whether we have solutions in life or just answers. The Lord's Prayer – Revisited gives us the understanding we need to examine the enemy's front line of offense: self—and its undercover role in the attacks against our lives. The Lord's Prayer disrupts the plans of the wicked and scatters the enemy of our soul **seven** *ways.*

We invite you to visit our website at:
Anointed Life Publishing

www.anointedlifepublishing.com

To get information regarding having Carolyn Chambers speak at your group, church, or organization, please e-mail us at:

carolyn.allow@yahoo.com

www.ingramcontent.com/pod-product-compliance
Lightning Source LLC
Chambersburg PA
CBHW070549300426
44113CB00011B/1839